Freight Broker Business Startup

The Ultimate Guide to Starting and Running a Trucking Freight Brokerage Business

© **Copyright 2018**

All rights Reserved. No part of this book may be reproduced in any form without permission in writing from the author. Reviewers may quote brief passages in reviews.

Disclaimer: No part of this publication may be reproduced or transmitted in any form or by any means, mechanical or electronic, including photocopying or recording, or by any information storage and retrieval system, or transmitted by email without permission in writing from the publisher.

While all attempts have been made to verify the information provided in this publication, neither the author nor the publisher assumes any responsibility for errors, omissions or contrary interpretations of the subject matter herein.

This book is for entertainment purposes only. The views expressed are those of the author alone, and should not be taken as expert instruction or commands. The reader is responsible for his or her own actions.

Adherence to all applicable laws and regulations, including international, federal, state and local laws governing professional licensing, business practices, advertising and all other aspects of doing business in the US, Canada, UK or any other jurisdiction is the sole responsibility of the purchaser or reader.

Neither the author nor the publisher assumes any responsibility or liability whatsoever on the behalf of the purchaser or reader of these materials. Any perceived slight of any individual or organization is purely unintentional.

Contents

INTRODUCTION	1
CHAPTER 1: INTRODUCTION TO FREIGHT TRUCKING BROKERAGE	2
CHAPTER 2: BROKER TRAINING AND INDUSTRY EXPERIENCE	6
CHAPTER 3: ROLE AND RESPONSIBILITIES OF A FREIGHT BROKER	14
CHAPTER 4: LICENSING AND BUSINESS REGISTRATION	24
CHAPTER 5: START A HOME-BASED FREIGHT BROKER BUSINESS	38
CHAPTER 6: TIPS AND ADVICE FOR YOUR FREIGHT BROKER FIRM	48
CHAPTER 7: MARKETING AND FINDING CLIENTS	56
CHAPTER 8: TIPS FOR BECOMING A SUCCESSFUL FREIGHT BROKER	65
CONCLUSION	85

Introduction

The following chapters will discuss everything you need to know about being a freight broker and how you can start your own firm. All chapters of this book are essential and will take you through a step-by-step journey into becoming a licensed and registered freight broker.

In the first two chapters, you will learn about the role of a freight broker. To establish a freight broker business, you will need to gain industry experience, get a license from the federal government and undertake numerous other processes.

This book is a step by step guide to becoming a successful freight broker with a large number of clients who bring about good profit. Every effort was made to ensure that it was full of as much useful information as possible.

Chapter 1: Introduction to Freight Trucking Brokerage

In the broader transport sectors, a variety of people who need shipping like business owners, distributors, and suppliers of goods and services sign contracts with trucking companies to transport goods to intended destinations. However, there is still a significant quantity of freight that is managed by freight brokers. Truck brokering aims to maximize the profits acquired through freight hauling as they facilitate lucrative cargo hauling interactions between freight companies and trucking firms.

Who is a Freight Broker?

A freight broker is an expert who acts as the mediator between a trucker and carrier with the capacity and ability to move cargo that needs transporting.

The Need for Freight Brokerage Services

As mentioned, goods are transported by transport companies that have a contract agreement with freight companies. However, there are numerous instances where cargo needs shipping but no trucks are available. Consider this: a trucker receives a call for a huge amount of cargo. Unfortunately, all their trucks have already departed to various destinations. If taken care of, huge amount of income can be made for this additional load to be transported. In such instances, freight brokers come in handy.

How to Make Money as a Truck or Freight Broker

A registered freight or truck broker builds relationships with trucking companies to easily handle moving freight cargo. If your truck company runs out of available vehicles for shipping, the broker would lease the additional cargo to another transporter and then receive a small commission in the process.

As a general rule, trucking companies often negotiate their own cargo. If they have an insufficient number of trucks, they lose the chance of transporting the additional cargo as well as the opportunity to broker the new shipment to another transport firm.

Opportunities Abound in the Freight and Tracking Sector

To be completely honest, it is a great time to become a freight broker these days.

With the continuing evolution of technology and the internet age, the opportunities for any interested individual to start their own brokerage business grows.

In the past couple of years, the US economy improved significantly. With it comes the growth and expansion of the logistics and transport industry, therefore, an increased demand for freight brokers.

Generally, A Freight Brokerage business has strong potential profit-wise. All experts in the transport and logistics industry agree that now is the perfect time to begin a freight brokering company, with a possible income of at least $90,000 a year. Also, freight brokerage companies are indispensable in the goods and cargo transport industry. Basically, such firms keep the industry going. If you are reading this with an interest of learning how to begin your own freight brokering firm, read away and begin to work as soon as possible.

Starting your own Truck Brokering Business

Before starting any business, it is advisable to learn as much about the industry as possible. For instance, what does trucking involve? What are the licensing or registration requirements? You need, of course, clear answers to all of these questions before you begin. You will also need to understand what the role of a freight broker is within the broader transport industry.

Compliance

One of the most crucial aspects of the truck brokerage business is compliance. As with all industries, there are rules, regulations, and requirements. If you learn how to comply with these rules, then you will get off to a great start.

Procedures such as late renewal penalties, bond claims, and consumer complaints that can deplete your money and time can be avoided by keeping yourself informed and secure. Complying with regulations is extremely important as the truck broker industry grows again. The number of freight brokers has been growing each year steadily by about 1,000 per year since 2014. At the start of 2015, there were slightly over 15,000 licensed freight brokers in the US. This figure rose to slightly above 16,000 in 2016, and in January of 2017, the number had grown to 17,012.

This steady growth over the last couple of years is due to one main reason: A steady increase in local freight volumes within the United States and also, an increase in export and import cargo. This steady increase in cargo business calls for more players in the sector, especially trucking brokers. Your efforts in choosing this path will help to move increasing freight volumes across the US and overseas.

Legal Requirements

Starting your own freight brokerage career is relatively straightforward. Like any other business, you will need to fulfill some legal requirements, especially getting bonded and acquisition of an operating license. If you are a new to the industry, ample training as well as direct industry experience. This will help you understand how to set up your business as well as all your legal obligations and requirements that will ensure you remain compliant.

It is important to acquire all the necessary information to guide you through the entire process. This book is precisely created to be an excellent resource for all aspiring trucking brokers.

Chapter 2: Broker Training and Industry Experience

Broker Training

Basically, broker training is not compulsory, and no one will ever ask if you attended a particular class or training program. However, you will benefit immensely by attending a training course that will inform, educate, and familiarize you with the workings, duties, responsibilities, and official roles of a transport broker. Training is highly recommended so you can also learn other tricks and tips that will enable you to identify the leading carriers and shippers you should partner with. It also gives you exactly what you need to know in terms of the legal requirements of this business. It is important to stay at right side of the law at all times: this begins by having the business registered in your state then later on, seeks a federal license from the Federal Motor Carrier Safety Administration (FMCSA). Receiving the necessary training and education will not hurt as it will help you become a more competent practitioner and will have the edge over all others who chose not to attend any training at all.

To get started, there are some free broker training courses that you can find online. However, these are very basic. Comprehensive freight brokerage courses can range from $150 to over $3,000, depending on the length and complexity of the course. Some training courses, mostly those at the high end, may even offer to link you with a freight brokerage so that you gain hands-on experience.

Freight Broker Training Schools

If you are keen, you may also consider freight broker training schools. Each training school offers a different but targeted course that is aptly tailored for freight brokers. Not only do the schools offer training but they also provide materials and training packages that will enable you to practice in your own free time.

Free Training Resources for Freight Brokers:

- *Export Tutorials* – offered by Michigan State University

- *Logistics Systems* – a free course offered at MIT

- *Import and Export Training Videos* – offered by US Census Bureau

- *Introduction to Transportation Systems* – free course at MIT

As a broker, you will need some industry-specific skills out in the field. There is basically no substitute for this. You will require lots of diligence and practical experience. For this, persistence, practice and strong will to learn the ins and outs of the business will get you ahead of the game.

Math and Business Skills

It shouldn't be surprising that in this business, you must work hard to learn or refresh your math and arithmetic skills as these are the skills that you will use the most on a daily basis. As a freight broker, you will be working with numbers in different facets, forms and this will require critical thinking and proper analysis to benefit from all existing opportunities.

Communications Skills

A huge part of this job is include negotiations and deal closing. This business will require and put you in positions to be in constant communication with others within the freight and trucking industry. Therefore, your people skills need to be up to speed, especially via email or telephone.

Education

Educating yourself constantly is key. You should also expect to gain valuable and practical knowledge regarding the functions and responsibilities in time by taking notes of each situation you've encountered so far. You will also need to go through the Broker Operation Manual that contains all the data and theoretical info that is essential for any expert broker. Then you will need to put aside at least one week to get some hands-on training at a trucking firm or brokerage so that you may develop some aforementioned essential skills.

Through experience, you will eventually learn how to negotiate fair and affordable shipping rates and how to relate well with shipping companies. Also remember that proper training can lead to professional job openings. There are plenty of logistics, transport, and shipping companies that could use the consultation services of a well-trained expert.

Experts say that training should not take any more than three weeks. Only this much time is needed to learn all the theory, coursework, and plenty of hands-on experience.

Useful Tips for a Successful Freight Brokerage Career

As you go further into this book, you realize there are plenty of things that you need to learn to work competently as a freight broker. Fortunately, other experienced brokers have come up with some tips and pieces of advice:

First, it is about understanding a customer's needs and desires. As the popular saying goes, *"the customer is always right"*, is something you should take into account every day. Always keep in mind that there are plenty of other brokers out there hoping to take your client. Also remember that there are over 14,000 brokerages and 500,000 trucking firms across the United States. If you do not show them how you care about their welfare and show that you have their best interest at heart, they could easily find someone else who can.

Get to know your clients on a more personal level. Build a professional but friendly relationship, know what they care about and use it as leverage – Try and address your clients in the same way you would friends or family, and avoid switching to a tone that is too business or money driven. Keep in close contact with all of your clients. It is important that you are the first person the client thinks about when they have an extra load that needs to be shipped out at the last minute.

Set high standards for reliable word and affordable transportation rates. Give sufficient information that they need to make a decision. That way, they will be pleased and will come back to you on a regular basis. Pay close attention to both what your client says and what they don't say. For instance, do they seem agitated? Do they seem upset, worried, or bothered? If so, then you do not have to bother them. Instead, ask if it is the right time to talk or should the discussions be postponed to a later date.

Create a community based form of sharing information. Find out from your clients if they regularly send out email lists of all their available freight. If so, then you should request to have your email included just so that you do not miss out on any opportunities in the future, or for a more modern twist, suggest Facebook or chat groups to keep everyone in the loop.

Lastly, as a trucking broker, never take any freight that you cannot move. This can result in a disastrous situation. It never hurts to play safe than taking on something you can't handle in the long run.

Learn How to Prepare for Negotiations

Generally, negotiations made in person are different from those made over the phone. You will fare well if you prepare for phone negotiations as these will be the most common.

First, ensure that you properly understand what your terms and targets are. Next, think about how you will convince your clients to accept your terms. Most importantly, always leave room for negotiations –most clients will try and negotiate the fees.

Some clients will ask a lot of questions, and it is an essential part of the job to be prepared with answers. Apart from the clients, transport and shipping partners will also have sets of questions for any freight that your customers wish to transport. Remain confident as you answer. Coherent speech in a friendly tone will always win over the other person. Remember that when you stumble, you appear weak and indecisive, so make sure that you are always prepared. You are the expert in this business; therefore, you should sound like it.

Do your Due-Diligence

As a dedicated broker, you must ensure that you get all the information necessary from the shippers or transporters. This information will come in handy when you provide information to your clients or vice versa.

You will also need to get as much information about the package from your client as possible. This information will enable your transporters to provide you with accurate rates, time, and so on. Sometimes transporters call clients directly when you do not have an answer they need. You do not want to be in this situation, so do your due diligence and acquire all the essential information needed.

Be Smart

Posting your freight on the load boards is not enough. This is simply another way of telling them that you do not actually have the freight with you. This is often a sign of weakness and incompetence – something you would never want your partners to experience.

Instead, take time to search and find trucks that are within 100-150 miles of your location then start contacting them. It is better to allow some time so that your client is ready by the time the truck arrives.

Multi-tasking when you are in negotiations with the traffic manager, a driver, or a dispatcher is not ideal. When you try to multi-task, even simple tasks like sending an email or opening a page can hinder you from providing the transporter with accurate information. Eliminate simple errors by focusing on the task at hand and ensuring the information relayed to the transporters is accurate. If emails, phones, or computers cause a distraction, then turn them off when the call comes in.

Important Points to Note

As a freight broker, you should be meticulous in everything you do, sustaining a high level of organization and proper communication amidst the chaos and busy nature of the job. Therefore, if take notes (digital or handwritten) of people you have called, packages you need to move and so on.

Information to be forwarded to Truck Companies

There are certain things that you as a freight broker, need to forward to the trucking company. In fact, relaying this information to your transport partners is crucial. These include:

- Load destination
- Load origin

- Specific commodity
- Total loading miles
- Total weight
- Loading hours
- Unloading hours
- Required equipment
- Rate

If you take note and handle the above responsibilities with utmost importance, then you will be on your way to becoming a successful and respected freight broker.

Training to Become an Expert Truck Broker

We have already established that freight brokers are the mediators of the transport supply chain. The trucking and logistics industry in America is worth about $1.5 trillion as of 2015. A lot of cargo is hauled by pipelines, water, and railway across the USA. However, a majority of freight is transported via road so there will always be a demand for this.

Moving Ahead Progress (MAP-21)

An Obama-era transportation law known as MAP-21 was introduced in July of 2012. This introduced new and significant changes to the transport sector. It essentially increased the barriers for entering into the trucking industry.

What the MAP-21 does is introduce higher fees when it comes to bonding which simply kicks out truckers and freight brokers from the industry. However, the benefit of this law is that it has reduced the number of freight brokers in the industry, opening the room for more serious and determined players.

The Freight Broker

There are many different titles used in the industry to refer to a freight broker. Other popular titles include truck broker, transportation broker, transportation intermediary, or logistics consultant.

As a mediator between shippers or clients and carriers, your main purpose as a truck broker is to actually negotiate great rates for your clients and ensure their goods or products are delivered to the desired destination with no delays and zero damage.

To negotiate rates, you will need to work with the shipper. As soon as you agree on a rate, you will then proceed to negotiate rates with transporters. A broker must also organize the collection of the freight by the transporter and ensure that it is sent to its intended destination as soon as possible.

It is expected that, with time, you will build strong and lasting relationships with clients or shippers and with transport and logistics companies. As a broker, you will choose whether to manage all your documentation in a soft or hard copy. Some prefer all documentation in the form of paper while others prefer to go digital with a freight broker software.

Things like gadgets including computers, printers, fax machines, and cellphones are essential. The nature of a broker's job is more often than not, an office job, and you will mostly operate from there without the need to get out in the field.

Chapter 3: Role and Responsibilities of a Freight Broker

Job Description of a Freight Broker

It is important that you understand the role of a freight broker and what is expected of this crucial logistics and transport expert. Essentially an expert in the logistics and transport sector who liaises between shippers and transporters, the main responsibility of the freight broker is to negotiate favorable shipping rates as well as speedy delivery times with the transport companies. As a broker, you should always work with the client to ensure that you get them the best shipping rates. To arrive at an acceptable figure, both of you will negotiate. You will find that after a couple of weeks or months, you will develop close and cordial working relations with your clients.

Responsibilities

It is the responsibility of a freight broker to ensure that cargo is booked, collected, transported appropriately, and eventually delivered. It is also your responsibility as a trucking broker to communicate effectively with both clients and shippers to ensure that cargo is moved fast and effectively from its original location to its final destination.

On previous chapters, we've mentioned the essential information that needs to be given to the They need this information as early as possible to arrange for collection and shipment. The cargo that your transporters collect may travel by road, ship, and sometimes air.

Cargo Delivery is the Broker's Responsibility

On most occasions, freight brokers never get to see the cargo being moved. However, they assume responsibility for its safe and speedy delivery, as well to ensure that every aspect of the cargo shipment flows smoothly. This is why you need all the training as well as access to sophisticated computer software and systems. These will enable you to track shipments at every stage so that your clients can follow the delivery of their goods. Remember that you will be dealing with multiple clients and not just one client; hence the need for computer systems.

You need to get a License

To carry out broker duties efficiently, you will have to be licensed. All truck brokers are licensed by any one of a number of government agencies. These include the Federal Maritime Commission and the Federal Motor Carrier Safety Administration which falls under the US Department of Transport. Freight brokers can also seek registration from the Transportation Security Administration. This one is for managing air freight cargo. Getting licensed with the appropriate government agency is one of the first things that you should seek to achieve before you begin work. Clients definitely prefer working with registered agents for their own safety and well-being.

A Freight Broker Provides Excellent Business

Freight brokers provide an invaluable service to both clients and transporters. They facilitate transporters and help them to fill up their trucks with cargo. This reduces the transporters' costs and earns the freight broker a commission for their hard work. There are plenty of transport companies that use brokers to help find shippers. Such companies often give the freight brokers a free hand to totally coordinate all the transport and shipping operations.

Brokers since Early 1900s

These type of brokers have been around since the start of the 1900s. However, there were plenty of regulatory and legal hurdles that restricted interested companies and individuals from actively working as truck brokers. Such restrictions hampered the industry until the early 1970s.

Before then, very few firms were willing to attempt to enter the industry. However, with the easing of regulatory restrictions and major changes in the federal transport policy, more players have ventured into the truck brokering industry.

Participants in the Logistics and Transport Sector

The logistics and transport industry is huge and diverse. Numerous players enable it to grow and thrive. It is imperative that you can identify the different players in the industry to know whom to contact and who does what. Sometimes roles can overlap, and at other times the titles of the different experts can be confusing. However, with time, you should be able to identify all the individual experts in the industry.

To start you off, here is a list of some of the major players in the sector:

Freight Broker: A mediator who brings together carriers and shippers.

Carrier: This is a firm that transports cargo. There are basically two types of carriers: Private firms and those that are up for hire. Private firms usually transport their own cargo. For-hire companies are paid to deliver freight services to others.

Shipper: A shipper is a client, either a business or individual, with cargo that needs to be transported.

Freight Forwarder: These are experts who take actual, physical charge of goods and then consolidate many other shipments together to constitute one big shipment. The forwarders, who are often mistaken for freight brokers, then organize transport via different modes like air and road.

Export-Import Broker: This expert mostly facilitates processes for importers and exporters. They usually work closely with government agencies, such as customs control, major international carriers, and other companies, to facilitate the movement of goods into and out of a country.

Shippers Association: This is a non-profit cooperative organization often founded by shippers. The main aim of the association is to help members lower the transport prices. They do this by pooling together their cargo. The shipper's associations operate in a very similar manner to freight forwarders associations. However, their services are unavailable to the general public and limited to members only.

Agriculture Truck Brokers: These are truck brokers who are fairly small in number yet limited to certain geographical regions of the country. Most of the time, these brokers organize transportation for agriculture produce that is exempt.

If we existed in a perfect world, then each of these specialized experts would focus on their traditional role, and that would be it.

Today, however, the world has changed drastically over the last couple of decades. This has resulted in blurred lines resulting in most experts venturing into other specialties. It is also a very common occurrence for truck brokers to expand their businesses through the creation of additional companies and subsidiaries providing freight services.

Essentials of an Effective Freight Broker

As a broker, you can assimilate yourself into any industry and not just transport and logistics. Some of the most successful freight brokers also go into auto and mortgage businesses.

The most successful freight brokers are those experienced in sales and customer service. Interpersonal relationships are a crucial aspect for successful brokers. This is probably why mortgage and car brokers are usually the successful ones in the transport sector. They have the necessary people skills and understand how to interact with clients. If you are new to this industry, you can always learn the important industry skills as these can be taught.

Using Agents

Sometimes brokers prefer to work with agents whenever they want to develop additional operations. An agent is simply an independent contractor found in a specific area and represents the freight broker. This offers you a great way to have a presence in regions other than where you are located. Such an arrangement will come in handy especially when you do not have the volumes that would justify opening a fully-fledged office.

If you are an aspiring broker, then you will fare much better if you connect with a brokerage company. Such a connection will provide you with the best chance yet to build relations and interact with clients. A good brokerage firm will ensure that you have access to good quality tools, equipment, software, and all other things that a broker needs. Such a firm needs to be flexible as well as financially stable.

Case in point is the freight brokerage firm Trangistics. The firm is based in Oregon even though it has agents all over the U.S., including Nevada, California, Texas, Alaska, Illinois, Alabama, Georgia, North Carolina, among others. Since the agents are not freight brokers, they often operate from a home office and only have access to a phone and computer. On most occasions, agents operate and function very similarly to how truck brokers function. The only difference is that agents operate under the auspices of the broker. The broker still retains the legal recognition, bond, and responsibility of ensuring cargo is transported on time.

An experienced freight broker will try and acquire liability insurance and contingent cargo coverage that ensure they are covered should the transporter's insurance fail. If you can acquire this kind of insurance cover your clients will tend to trust you more and be happy knowing that their freight is adequately covered.

Managing Finances

As a freight broker, you must pay transporters and carriers before you receive payment from your clients. For this reason, you will most likely require a line of credit. This line of credit could range anywhere from $250-$500,000.

As a truck agent, if you do not pay the trucks on time, then they will not be willing to transport any cargo for you in the future. Moreover, with no trucks willing to haul your freight, then you will be in serious trouble. Therefore, always ensure that you make timely payment for prompt shipment of cargo. The bottom line for any successful broker is to ensure that they have the necessary license and required documentation, sufficient insurance cover, and sound finances. If you do not meet these requirements, then transporters may start ignoring your calls, stop returning your emails, and even offer very high charges for their services.

Freight Broker's Role in Operations and Incurring Costs

The concept of freight brokerage is fairly simple: you receive a call from a shipper with cargo that needs to be moved. The next step is to complete your own internal procedures such as paperwork and so on. You then begin the process of identifying the most appropriate transporter who can handle the consignment. It is absolutely crucial that you set up an agreement with a transporter before sending them on an assignment.

Depending on your agreement with the carrier or transporter, you may need to add an addendum to the agreement. It is only after everything is agreed on paper that a driver will be dispatched. You should expect the transporters to call you and inform you when they pick up a consignment and when they eventually deliver it to its intended destination.

You should always take it upon yourself to call you transport partners so they can dispatch a driver at the earliest opportunity. It is absolutely advisable that the driver should call you as soon as they pick up the cargo and have it in the truck. This way, you can then call your clients or shippers and let them know that the load has been picked up and what the expected delivery time is.

The driver should also call you once the cargo is delivered. This is important because you will need to note it down and enter it into your schedule. You will also need to notify the client once the goods are delivered. Fortunately, there are digital tools and software programs that enable you to track these down digitally. Most clients see this option as the most convenient one as it gives them freedom to check on the status of their cargo. As soon as the shipment is delivered, your transporter will send a bill of lading and an invoice. His makes the process more efficient.

Keep Meticulous Records

As a freight agent, you need to ensure that your note taking and record keeping skills are phenomenal. These are crucial. In fact, there are certain requirements regarding the types of records you need to maintain. These are specified by the Code of Federal Regulations. An agent is supposed to keep what is known as a master list of favorite shippers and carriers. This way, he or she will avoid repeating information. However, as the freight broker, you need to ensure that you maintain a record of each transaction. This is a requirement; ensure that you adhere to it. You should ensure that you hold onto these records for at least three years

Your records must be meticulous and should include all of the following information:

- Freight bill number or the bill of lading

- The address, registration number, and name of the originating carrier

- Your shipper's name and address

- The compensation amount received for the service offered

- The payer's details such as name and phone number

- Any additional, non-brokerage services offered for each shipment

- Any payment received for the non-brokerage services offered

- Name and contact information of the payer

- The amount of the freight charges that you collect as a broker

- The dates that you made payments to your transporters

As mentioned several times in this book, you are the expert in the industry. These will save you from potential trouble in the future.

Physical Address

It is often a great relief to anyone joining the transport industry as a freight agent to find out that physical startup needs are usually very small. Other experts like freight forwarders and transport require a loading dock, warehouses, and trucks. However, as a freight broker, you will require none of these.

In most instances, your clients will not need to come to your premises. So you do not need to spend hundreds of dollars sprucing up your office with expensive furniture and décor or a reception area. This means you can be located just about anywhere you wish, even at your own home. The office that you operate from will depend on things such as your goals for your firm as well as your budget. Many agents begin their businesses at home-based offices with the hope of later upgrading to a formal office once they are properly established.

One of the major benefits of starting out at a home office is that the minimal cost. However, there are many other things that you will need to consider. For instance, does your house have a separate space that can be used as an office? This area will need to be quiet, away from the kids, guests, and pets. You will need to set up a proper and professional workstation where you will operate from productively with no distractions.

Setting up a commercial office is obviously more costly. You will need plenty of resources to meet the essential costs such as overheads, rent money, lease deposit, and so on. However, it is worth it. You will eventually find out that commercial space allows a much more efficient layout and setup for your work compared to a spare room at your residence.

Your Income

As a mediator and problem solver in the transport and logistics industry, you can expect to receive adequate remuneration for your efforts. A bulk of your income will come from the freight fees that you charge. These charges are often based upon a number of variables. However, the major factors that determine freight charges include trailer space, distance, and cargo weight.

Sometimes the freight charges will depend on the type of transport system necessary for the job. Refrigerated trucks, for instance, charge a much higher rate compared to regular flatbed trucks. Rates are affected if a truck driver has to stop more than once to collect or deliver cargo. Each shipment is ideally entitled to at least one pickup stop and one delivery at no additional costs. However, any additional stops can be charged at rates that can be negotiated and agreed upon with the transport company. As a freight broker, you should be conversant with the latest freight or shipping rates before engaging a transport company or a shopper. Remember that your income is based on the margin so be careful with your charges.

Chapter 4: Licensing and Business Registration

Now that you have gained necessary education and industry experience, you need to move to the next level. The crucial initial steps of setting up your business will involve getting licensed and getting your business registered. To accomplish these tasks, you will need to fill out some paperwork. The process will include:

• Registering your business with the state government

• Applying for a license with the federal government

• Taking out an essential surety bond that covers against unseen hazards

Fortunately, all these processes can be done and completed online. If you have a credit card, a connected computer, and resources to get a hold of all other required forms and fees, then you will be able to accomplish these crucial yet straightforward steps within a few minutes.

<u>Federal Licensing Requirements</u>

Any brokers that ship merchandise across state lines need to seek authorization from the federal government. The arm of the federal government that is responsible for registering freight brokers is the

Federal Motor Carrier Safety Administration (FMCSA). When you submit your application forms as well as a small processing fee, you should receive your license within four-six weeks.

Before the year 2015, brokers had to fill out a number of forms and then submit them to the FMCSA either via post or email. However, things have changed since then. What you need to do is make use of the Unified Registration System (URS). The URS puts together all the forms that you need to sign to streamline the application process.

1. Apply for the Operating Authority

One of the initial steps of seeking federal licensing is the application for the operating authority. This is also referred to as the MC number and simply the authority granted to you by the federal government to work as a freight broker. The federal government has an elaborate Unified Carrier Registration process for freight brokers with agents across different cities or towns. You will need to designate an agent or representative within each state where you operate. The federal government normally issues two types of operating authorities:

- Authority for household goods brokers
- Authority for property brokers

To be on the safe side, you should apply for both types of operating authorities, and the good news is, you are actually allowed to do so. Each costs approximately $300. During the license application process, the federal government will request certain information such as:

- Personal and contact information
- Social security number
- Employer identification number

Sometimes the government requires you to obtain a USDOT number if you intend to act as a motor carrier. Therefore, it's best to be ready for this step during the licensing process.

2. Receive a Grant Letter and MC/FF Number

As soon as your application is received and processed, you will receive a MC/FF number. This number is also known as your operating authority granted by the federal government. You will need this number most of the time as you execute your duties. However, even at this stage, you won't have completed the entire process just yet.

First, the federal government, through the Department of Transport, will send you a grant letter. You will have to wait ten days, during which anyone could question your application. After that, you can begin the process of applying for surety bonds. Freight brokers often apply for the BMC-84 bond which is suitable for freight brokers. This is a type of financial protection that is worth $75,000. As a broker, this guarantees your clients compensation – should you fail to adhere to all laws and federal regulations governing the handling and transportation of cargo. Your clients will be free to file a claim for compensation if your actions cause loss or damages.

As a freight broker, you will obtain bonds through agencies such as Lance Surety Bonds. They often collaborate with bond companies that issue the bonds and then back them with financial muscle. During the bond application process, the bond agency will offer you a quote which refers to the cost at which your bond can be obtained. Certain factors will determine this cost. These include certain financial indicators such as your personal credit score. The normal rates range from 1-5% of the total bond amount, usually $75,000.

Once your bond application is approved, the bond company then informs the FMCSA. You will also have the option of entering into a

Trust Fund Agreement instead of the surety bond. However, you will have to contribute the full amount of $75,000 to the fund. Most new brokers find this to be a huge challenge, and it tends to lock up financial resources that could be utilized in other ways.

When searching for a suitable bond agency to get a bond, make sure that the chosen agency is affiliated with T-listed and A-rated companies. Such companies are considered financially stable, reliable, and will guarantee to stand by you in case one of your clients files a claim.

3. Apply for Freight Broker Insurance Cover

The freight broker insurance cover is not a mandatory obligation required by law, especially if you intend to operate only as a broker. It is only a requirement for operators who wish to acquire forwarding or carrier authority.

However, while insurance is not a requirement for freight brokers, it is highly recommended. This is because in the course of executing your duties, something may get damaged or lost and you may be held personally responsible. In such cases, the insurance will come in handy. The types of insurance often taken out by truck brokers include liability insurance, property insurance, and cargo insurance. It is especially important to have coverage since some carriers may not purchase insurance for the cargo they are transporting.

Also, when you eventually employ at least two workers, then you will need to acquire workers' compensation insurance. This type of cover is necessary and mandatory for all employers in all states. This is regardless of the type of business that is being undertaken.

Ensure that you confirm with your carriers if they have appropriate insurance cover. There are a number of cases where freight brokers have been sued or pursued for workers' compensation, and successfully so, by employees of carrier companies even when these employees did not work for the brokers. Unless state regulations exempt them from workers' compensation cover, they should have appropriate cover for their workers.

4. Ensure that you Designate Process Agents

As soon as you obtain your FF/MC number, you should then designate your process agents. Your agents need to be designated for each state that you plan to open an office or at least where you intend to have contracts. You are allowed to be an agent within your own state where you have your office and are based. If no one protests your application within the designated protest period, and you were able to comply with all the federal government's requirements, then the FCMSA will proceed to issue you with your freight broker license which will be your operating authority.

If at this point, you have managed to officially become a licensed freight broker, congratulations!

Financial Implications of Becoming a Freight Broker

Are there any huge costs associated with becoming a broker? Inevitably, there are and always will. Here are some costs you need to watch out for:

- Insurance policies
- Operating authority
- Business registration
- Freight broker bond
- Broker training
- Business location and equipment
- Manpower and miscellaneous expenses

These kinds of costs are likely to vary depending on different factors. However, we have taken the time to put a number beside these words:

1. Business Registration

Business registration prices vary in each state. However, according to the Small Business Administration, you can expect to pay roughly between $150-$300 to have your business registered.

2. Operating Authority or License

Expect to pay about $300 for each authority that you wish to change or acquire. For instance, if you wish to get a license as a freight broker and a freight forwarder, then you will pay $300 for each license.

3. Freight Broker Bond Costs

Please note that you will also be required to make some payments for your bond. As it is, the cost of the bond varies and is determined on an individual basis. There are annual premiums to be paid, and these are based on the following factors:

- Experience in the industry
- Financial muscle
- Your credit score

Freight brokers with sufficient experience and excellent credit can expect to pay an annual $900-$3,750 per year. Those with little or no experience and poor credit scores can expect to pay much higher rates, possibly going up to $7,500.

It is advisable to note that the priced offered by different bond companies regularly fluctuates due to competition, losses and changing market conditions. If you want to obtain the best rates in the market, then you should consider signing up with an agency that represents a number of surety bond firms. Such firms can make a comparison of rates across different bond companies and then advise you on the best rates in the market.

Firms such as Lance Surety can provide you with a long list of bond rates as it represents multiple firms. This bond agency has strong relationships with a number of top bond companies that write Freight Broker Bonds. You will be able to obtain very competitive rates if you work with such an agency.

It is important to understand that even those with a poor credit rating can still receive bond. While the rate may not be the same as of those with good ratings, you will still have access to a bond and can proceed with your freight brokerage business. Do not hold yourself back just because you did not get a break.

Cost of Claims

There are other costs that you need to consider besides bond premiums. Your bond's true cost does not just consist of the premiums that you pay annually. It also includes the total amount of liability that could result from any claims filed against you. Should any claims be paid out concerning your bond, then you will most likely be liable to repay the bond company. In most extreme cases, the amounts can be as high as $75,000 plus any associated legal fees.

This is the reason why it is crucial for freight brokers to partner with reliable and trustworthy bond agencies that will treat you with respect and act in your best interest should a claim be made. A reputable bond company will support you all through the bond process including helping to deal with any claims that are filed.

Insurance Policies

Insurance cover is necessary but not mandatory. If you choose to get cover such as contingent cargo insurance, then you can expect annual costs that range from $1,200 to around $1,600. Another type of insurance that you are likely to require is workers' compensation. If you decide to opt for general liability insurance instead, then your insurance costs may rise to about $3,000 annually.

Insurance and other costs are difficult to predict as they will largely depend on your plans for your brokerage firm. However, you can save costs if you adopt some cost-saving measures. For instance, you can work from a home office instead of leasing commercial office space.

And when you start your home office, ensure that you use the home telephone and computer for your work in order to cut back costs. However, you really should invest in good quality broker software that will enable you to operate professionally. A good transport management system can cost approximately $600-$1,200 per annum. Even then, it is bound to be earning a pretty decent income, so it is worth the investment.

Registering and Starting your Freight Brokerage Business

Now that you have all the necessary instruments to operate a freight brokerage business, the next step is to register your business with the state authorities. You will need to form your own Limited Liability Company or LLC. You need to understand how the process goes so that you can do it yourself with ease. If you find the process too challenging or complex, then you can hire a lawyer for some advice. preferably the ones who specializes at drafting and setting up businesses. However, we think that the process is pretty simple and straightforward. See the steps below:

1. Identify a suitable business name that conforms to the state's business registration rules.

2. Prepare your paperwork by filling out all the necessary forms and providing all the required information, including personal details and contact information.

3. Once the paperwork is ready, submit it all together with all required attachments. Accompany the paperwork with the required fees. The fees can range anywhere from $100-$800 depending on the rules and your state.

4. Now come up with a suitable LLC operating agreement which role is to indicate the rights and responsibilities of LLC members. Once these are published, you then need to publish a notice of intent that lets the general public known that you wish to form an LLC. Follow this procedure only if it is a requirement in your state.

5. Once your business is registered, you can then proceed to apply for other licenses and permits necessary for operations.

The Business Registration Process

The process of registering your business begins at the office of the Secretary of State within your state. The registration procedures will vary from state to state. However, the process generally begins with your secretary of state's office.

Sometimes you may be required to head over to the local tax office, at the Department of Revenue, to register as a taxpayer. Business tax registration is crucial if you are to operate legally, as required. When registering your business, you will not be limited only to a Limited Liability Company. There are other options available as well. They include the following:

- Partnership
- Sole proprietorship
- Corporation
- Limited liability company

As you choose the best fit for your business, remember that there is no wrong or right choice. What matters is identifying the most suitable form of business that you require.

Learn About Truck Load Boards

A load board or freight board is a matching system online that lets freight brokers and shippers post loads. The boards also provide for transporters or carriers to post any free equipment in their possession. This makes it easy for carriers and shippers to find each other and then draft agreements that enable them to work together to move cargo.

Many of these load boards are sophisticated platforms. They allow users, shippers, brokers, and transporters, to search or post loads using a particular criterion. The load boards also provide additional services to carriers and freight brokers. Some of these additional services include the following:

- Message boards,
- FMCSA verification
- Load Matching
- Financing of pre-approved loads
- Capacity to note info on shippers and carriers
- Mobile access
- The necessary credit information

You can find a number of load or freight boards out there. Some are free while others charge a fee. The paid ones can be quite costly. You can expect to pay about $100 per month to gain access. Keep in mind that you get exactly what you pay for.

Just remember that paid load boards are not always the best so you should keep searching until you find the one that is perfect for your business.

While load boards are useful, they do have their pros and cons. For instance, if you are a new operator, you are likely to find lots of great opportunities on the board. However, the problem is that they have too many players and this tends to reduce margins and increase competition to unhealthy levels.

Factoring Invoices through the Load Board

Many load boards integrate loads together with firms that provide freight bill factoring. The integration enables freight brokers to take on slow-paying freights so it is a useful feature when you are running low on funds. You get access to crucial financing that can help you pay for any repairs, fuel, and the driver. You can also use the funds to take additional loads to expand your operations.

As a truck broker, you will often find that freight bills take pretty long to get settled. Sometimes even more than sixty days. In such instances, you may require finances to meet your regular or recurrent expenditure. This is where bill factoring comes in handy. It allows you to gain access to much-needed funds which you can use as you see fit. You can easily factor invoices through a load board. Here is how it is done:

Freight Bill Factoring Process

- Deliver a consignment to your client
- Then send an invoice to the client and a copy to the funder
- Once these are received, the advanced funds will be wired to you
- The transaction will then be completed once your client pays

What are the Benefits of Bill Factoring?

- You enjoy predictable funds access
- Approvals are often quite fast
- You have access to pay drivers, repairs, and fuels
- Sometimes it comes with fuel cards

Always ensure that you choose the correct factoring company to partner with. You should also find out how long it will take them to send you funds to finance your initial freight bill. All these are crucial when seeking a funding firm to engage with.

Negotiate the Best Terms

You should be able to engage the company and enter into negotiations to receive the very best terms. The profit margins in the transport sector are minimal, so it is difficult to find wiggle room. The margins are tight mainly due to stiff competition in the industry. Therefore, the costs will depend on:

- Your shippers and agents' credit
- Extra or additional fees
- Factoring rate
- Factoring advance

Once your business is up and running, you should ensure that you acquire the correct software. Good quality software can make a huge difference to your business. For instance, quality Transport Management Software (TMS) can help you manage your records and paperwork, plan routes appropriately, dispatch drivers, send invoices, and even set up shipping well in advance. Should a crisis arise, then you can use the tools provided to sort out the crisis.

You will be required to be online most of the time. Truck or freight brokering is as much about computers and the Internet as it is about consignments and deliveries. Online platforms such as the modern ones that you will be using are competing seriously with the traditional phone and fax machines. There are apps in the market today that you can use to help manage your business and increase efficiency. Unfortunately, some apps in the market are trying to eliminate brokers from the equation and trying to link consigners or shippers with transporters. Try and find shippers who use standardized shipments that require standard trucks. Sometimes you will need to get into direct contact with firms that provide specialized shipping.

Setting Up your Freight Brokerage Business

Now that you have completed most of the essential processes, you are more than ready to begin work. One of the most crucial steps you need to follow is to establish credibility. As a newcomer, no truck company or client will touch you with a ten-foot pole unless you can prove that you have the necessary authority as well as surety bonds. It is only after you are properly registered, licensed, and possess all the essential authority to operate as a freight broker that you begin getting clients and loads.

You will also need to get your finances in order. Many truckers are wary of freight brokers who dish out jobs but do not have the finances to pay for the service.

It is also important, if you feel the need, to start off as an agent. An agent is basically one who works for an established broker. You can be in a different location with your own office, but the experience is invaluable. Once you receive sufficient experience as an agent, you can then set up yourself as a freight broker. This also provides an excellent way of acquiring your own clients.

It is advisable to expect to hurt and lose money in the first year of business. Unless you are really good or have sufficient experience, a lot of new freight brokers barely break even in the first year. However, if you hang in there, you should start enjoying success. You should expect to foot your costs and expenses for a while so be prepared for that.

Legal Process Agents

Once your business picks up and you want to set up offices in another state, then you should get an agent. You will need an agent in each state to represent you there. Officially, they are referred to as legal process agents. You are required by law to register the legal process agents in each state where they operate. Agents are often registered with the federal government transport department through the FMCSA. You will need to fill out and submit form number BOC-3. You will be charged a processing fee of about $50 with each BOC-3 form that you submit.

Chapter 5: Start a Home-Based Freight Broker Business

Setting up your Home Office

When starting out as a freight broker, you really should start off with a home office. Not all businesses can be started from home; however, a freight brokerage firm can operate successfully from a home office. Many successful firms today started in basements and living rooms.

Setting up a home office is simple. You will need to designate a specific room within the home. You need to ensure that this room is set aside from the rest of the home, especially when you are working. For instance, you need to keep the kids away when you are working as well as pests or even guests.

Adopt a disciplined and official attitude when working so that others can let you work. No client wants to hear kids playing, dogs barking, or loud music when discussing business.

Essential Home Office Equipment

You will require specific equipment for your home office. If you already have basic pieces of furniture, such as an office desk and a comfortable, sturdy seat, then you are ready to get started.

1. Workstation

You will need a workstation in your home office. This is where you will primarily be working from. Get a large enough table or office desk as well as a high back chair. If you already have these at home, then you can use these as they will save you from buying new ones.

If you do not have an office desk and a high back chair, then you can easily find these being sold locally or online. You do not have to purchase the most expensive items on the market. Simply find a good quality, functional desk and chair and set these up as soon as you can.

2. Computer, Telephone, and Internet

You will spend most of your working hours on your workstation talking on the phone and using your computer. Therefore, get a dedicated office line instead of using the home phone line. This will set aside your private life from your work. It will not appear prudent for a client to call you only to speak to a family member.

Get a nice, modern, fast, and reliable computer for your work. A good computer is fast, has a large memory capacity and can handle large software programs and the various apps that you will need for your work.

Clear the Clutter

Make sure that your home office is devoid of any clutter such as knickknacks, old magazines, newspapers, and even electronics should be removed. These can easily cause a distraction and look unsightly. A cluttered space usually brings about a cluttered mind. However, if you have any items in mind that will motivate and inspire you, then you can add these to your office.

You should try as much as possible to be organized and stay that way. If you are organized, then you will be productive, creative, and efficient. However, if you are not organized, then you will be counterproductive and distracted. Distraction often comes from things such as incomplete tasks, loose papers, clutter, and so on.

To be organized, you should get a trash can, filing cabinet, and even a shredder for the office. These are simple items but will go a long way in getting you organized so that you are efficient in your work and can focus on delivering quality services to your clients. Some people are messy by nature, and that is easy to understand. If this is you, then it is okay to ask for assistance on how to stay organized.

Set your Office Hours

While standard office hours are between 9.00 am and 5.00 pm, you may want to experiment with your work hours. Since you are your own boss, then you are allowed to do this. A home-based job offers you the flexibility to choose your preferred hours. This way, you can create a balance between business and pleasure. You should create hours that suit you, and once these become agreeable with your schedule, you should share them with your family –it is important that they know when you are working and when you are free.

Make sure that you choose office hours when your body is rested and refreshed. You do not want to work when you are fatigued. Working when you are fresh ensures you are productive and can accomplish some of the most demanding tasks. Once you identify appropriate office hours, make sure that you stick to these.

Set up Business Savings and Checking Accounts

Keep personal and business finances separate. You may need to have both a savings and checking account for business. You also need to think about signing up for third-party payment processors, especially if you will be accepting credit card or online payments. You have plenty of options when it comes to bank accounts and payment options so shop around until you find something that you really like.

Get a Postal Address if Necessary

Sometimes you may need a postal address where you will receive all official communications. While this is not always necessary, it is a great option to think about. A postal address will get you to stand out as an organized broker and also an organized manager. You may choose to use the postal address for invoices, direct mailings, and company letterheads. This also allows you to keep your home or personal address separate from your business address.

Working from home has numerous advantages. You will have access to a standard office, but without the costs and overheads you would expect from a regular commercial office.

Book Keeping and Accounting

You need to keep in mind that there are backroom issues involving your truck brokering business. These include invoicing, bookkeeping, payables, and invoicing. If you are new to the world of business and accounting, then you had better fold your sleeves and start learning.

While you do not really have to use accounting software, it makes a lot of sense to use it because it makes things easier. You can organize your finances properly and also manage your firm's accounts a whole lot better.

If you want to get your accounts managed professionally, then you will need to use accounting software. One of the best and most widely used is QBS or QuickBooks from Microsoft. QuickBooks is easy to use, readily available, and best suitable for all types of businesses.

When using QuickBooks, you will come across the three main categories:

- Classes

- Charts of Accounts

- Items List

These three main categories constitute the backbone of your freight brokerage business. Classes generate expenses and income. The charts of accounts and items list are very closely related. One points to your source of finances while the other seeks money from your clients.

The charts of accounts constitute a collection of categories that inform the government about your sources of finance and how you spent your money. On the other hand, the items list informs clients about exactly what you are billing them for. It indicates the kinds of services that you provide to them. These two items are linked together in your accounts.

Classes inform you how the income was generated. If you are a freight broker, then you would set up your clients as a class. You would want to know how much each of your clients paid you. In the end, the final accounts statement will let you know how much money you made, how much your expenses were and what your profits margin are.

Invoicing Clients

As a service provider, your clients will be expecting a bill once the service has been satisfactorily delivered. When you invoice your clients, you want to provide them with detailed information about the services provided. For instance, you might charge a client for moving their cargo. Your clients often have a choice of payment methods and will choose one of four methods. These methods include:

- Flat fee payment

- Fee per mile

- Payment by the hundred weight

When invoicing your clients, you will need to spell out the fee payment method. The flat rate method is pretty obvious. You may, for instance, agree to deliver a package for a client to a particular destination at a fixed price.

Sometimes these are not the only charges to the client. Using accounting software such as QuickBooks will help you process all your income and payments and show you what your profits are, what taxes you need to pay and so on. However, you will need to set it up appropriately before you can begin using it productively.

Bookkeeping and Accounting

Many freight brokers know that they will be involved in some form of accounting and bookkeeping at some point in their business. One of the best places to begin is with the chart of accounts. This chart is essentially a listing of the entire accounting transactions that you might expect to encounter as a freight broker. The list can include some or all of the following:

- Your assets, such as accounts receivable and cash in the bank;
- Liabilities, such as accounts payable and also both income and expenditure are included;
- Income and expenditure, including payments to your shippers and your profits; and
- Expenses, such as loading board fees, office overheads, and telephone costs.

You should assign a certain code or number to each transaction so that it is easy to plug in the figures when doing your accounts. When these figures are entered into your accounting software, you will then receive a financial statement that will let you know about your firm's financial affairs.

Accounting Mistakes to Avoid

While we endeavor to work hard and do the best that we can, freight brokers sometimes tend to make mistakes that can be costly. You job generally keeps you very busy throughout the week so you might hardly have the time to do much else. Bookkeeping and accounting are core activities that you should do, so it is important that you get organized and undertake these activities well.

1. Do not Attempt to do everything

Some business owners often try to save money by doing all the core activities themselves. New freight brokers with little accounting knowledge may insist on doing all the accounting themselves or delegate the task to less experienced staff members or even a family member. While this can save you money in the short-term, some costly errors in the future could cost you huge losses. If you are well-established, you should hire a bookkeeper; otherwise, consult an accountant and get everything set up properly.

2. Stop Postponing Crucial Tasks

Managing a freight broker business is hard work. Many freight brokers are often so busy they forget to perform vital tasks such as bookkeeping. Important bookkeeping tasks such as credit card accounts and reconciling bank statements are crucial and should not be postponed unnecessarily. When you reconcile your bank statements, you receive an accurate picture of your financial position. Postponing such basic bookkeeping tasks can be easy, but the ramifications may hit home one day when you realize that your credit levels are unsustainable. With regular bookkeeping, you will be able to trace any lost checks, missing deposits or even fraudulent transactions.

3. Always Track Receivables and Invoices

If you wish to get paid for your hard work, then you should always account for your receivables. Getting paid should be a huge part of your focus so always focus on doing things that ensure you get paid. Payment means cash for you and your business. Your business needs money to foot bills, pay workers, and even pay transporters.

If you want to avoid delayed payments, then always focus on important matters such as tracking receivables and invoices. If you find that you are too busy sometimes, then you may want to consider something known as invoice factoring. Invoice factoring is the process of getting your invoices paid by a third party, usually a finance company, for a small fee. This will ensure that you get access to much-needed finances almost instantly.

4. Don't Ignore Liabilities

Liabilities often constitute the debt and other monies that you owe to others. Whenever you are doing your accounts, always cancel out any liabilities that have been paid. Ensure that they do not remain in the books after clearing pending payments. Should you forget to reverse liabilities after payments are made, then you will have a larger bill of liabilities, and this will give your business a bad name.

Ensure that you can accurately and properly do your bookkeeping. If not, then employ a bookkeeper, so they keep an eye on the finances for you. Also, try and ensure that you have an accounting firm or a CPA look over your accounts from time to time. Do not worry about their fees because this is a sound investment in your business.

5. Categorize your Expenses Accurately

Many new and inexperienced truck brokers, or their bookkeepers, often get confused and misplace certain expenses. Expenses should, therefore, be appropriately labeled to avoid any unnecessary confusion. When there are too many categories, it gives the wrong image to lenders and sureties. The general opinion will be that your books are not properly prepared. You should ensure that you set up an accounting system that is easy to use, straightforward, and devoid of errors. Sometimes it is easier to consult a CPA annually to avoid common mistakes like those mentioned.

6. Ensure Invoices contain all Essential Details

You must ensure that you provide all the necessary details in the invoices you intend to submit to your clients. There are various details needed based on your clients' preferred billing method. Ensure that you follow the proper invoicing mechanism as required.

7. Use Accounting Software Functions Appropriately

There are plenty of new business owners, including freight brokers, who invest in top-quality software but do not make use of all the useful features. This is because they never take the chance to learn how to use these features. If you have a bookkeeper or an accountant working for you, then this is probably not necessarily an issue for you.

However, if you are the accountant, then you should take the time to learn how certain accounting software works. The most popular software on the market currently is QuickBooks so learn all of the useful features. When used correctly, the right accounting software will provide you with a clear and accurate picture of your firm's finances and will also save you money.

Pros and Cons of Factoring Invoices

Companies that face financial challenges due to slow-paying clients often consider an option known as invoice factoring. Invoice factoring is a process where a business gets its invoices paid off by another company, usually a third party, at a certain rate.

Businesses use this option when they need funds to offset payments such as office overheads, salaries, and payment to transporters. This situation arises because some clients take too long to pay invoices. Most clients take about a month or longer to pay invoices while freight brokers pay transporters almost immediately. It is this need for cash that creates a challenge and necessitates invoice factoring.

Pros of Invoice Factoring to Freight Brokers

- Immediate access to finances
- You can pay your carriers
- You get power to dictate terms to your clients
- You can properly manage credit
- It is an easy way of gaining access to credit
- Invoice factoring provides short-term solutions
- The amount of credit can increase over time
- Your invoices act as collateral
- There is no need to give up any equity
- Even small businesses can access this line of credit

While there are numerous pros or advantages of invoice factoring, there are certain disadvantages. For starters, it does not provide a perfect solution. Here are some cons associated with it:

- It is a very costly line of credit
- It is a labor-intensive process
- Invoice factoring solves only a single problem
- Companies providing the finance will contact your clients
- Some clients may refuse to honor invoices

Chapter 6: Tips and Advice for Your Freight Broker Firm

Make your Freight Brokerage Business a Successful One

As you set up your freight brokerage business, you should know if you are doing much better than your peers in other industries, such as the property sector. If you can come up with innovative ways of doing business, then you are likely to gain an edge over both your rivals and the industry in general. You should consider implementing some or all of the following tips to be successful.

Design an Impressive Business Plan

One of the most crucial steps that you should take is outlining an excellent business plan that will see you overcome any possible challenges, beat the competition and thrive. To be successful, you really have to understand all aspects of the business.

Start by designing a practical, detailed, and complete business plan that encompasses all the various aspects of the business. This will include office setup and running costs, the necessary equipment such as software and so on. You should also include your long-term plans. This way, you will be able to focus on optimizing opportunities that exist within the industry. You will also be able to use this plan as your definite road or pathway to success. You can find out exactly how to go about this by using the online tool provided by the US Small Business Administration for easy business plan construction.

Make use of Smartphones

Smartphones have become very popular with people around the globe. They have become even more popular because of apps, or application programs. These apps are an excellent and invaluable source of information. You can use the information for business analysis purposes. Think about apps such as GPS tracking, confirmation, and even delivery apps. While these apps are definitely useful, think about other apps which are even better for your business. For instance, apps that help you manage fuel efficiency and so on are very useful. There are plenty of valuable logistics apps that you can use, so find which ones you need and make use of them.

Make use of Freight Management Software

Smartphones and all the mobile application programs are great for certain applications. However, they are not ideal for all functions. There are certain situations that proper software will provide you with much better and more reliable results. Freight management software provides you with functional and in-depth management solutions. Many of them remove any manual processes and help to manage multiple shipments all at the same time. The main aim of these software programs is to enable you to optimize your business and speed up processes for increased efficiency. You can use these software programs to produce customized reports that will inform you and your clients at each stage of the process.

Be Conscious and Aware of your Location

You should always have a location in mind when setting up a business. Therefore, think about the location of your suburb, neighborhood, community, and so on. You should think about other counties as well. Think about locating your business in an area with fast growth. Magazines such as *Forbes* have put together a list of some of the fastest-growing U.S. cities. These are some of the best places to locate new clients and also where freight brokerage businesses are likely to thrive.

Become a Proactive Entrepreneur

Since the industry is competitive, don't sit around and wait for new business to come to you. Instead, be proactive and get out of your comfort zone. Try and cut out an image of yourself as a go-getter. Ensure that you get out there and find the business. You should try and meet shippers, and when you do, let them know how organized, prepared, and committed a broker you are. If you adopt this attitude, you will definitely thrive.

Remember to also focus on your online profile. You should put up a company website and then possibly come up with a blog at a later date. Blogs are very user-friendly nowadays, and almost anyone can create one. If you become an active blogger, then you will raise your profile, and shippers and others will come to respect you as an industry expert. All this online activity will definitely attract more clients to your business.

Try and Identify a Niche

Conducting appropriate market analysis about the market is important. Research, analyze your data, and then make an informed decision based on your findings. The information or the conclusion that you come up with will show you whether you need to make any adjustments. Niche markets can be very lucrative and with limited participants so try and get into one if you can. Avoid taking the easy way and doing things in a mundane and average manner. Otherwise, you will never see any significant growth or achieve your full potential.

Keep Educating Yourself

It is crucial to keep educating yourself. We are very fortunate today to have the Internet. It translates to information right at our fingertips. There are also online classes that you can enroll in Find case studies or reports and try and learn from these. They will keep you informed about the latest in the world of logistics and transport and will provide you with numerous growth opportunities.

Think about your Clients' Needs

Many shippers often need to know whether you are licensed and bonded. They are very insistent on this fact, so it is important that you are legal with all the requirements. Shippers are also interested in plenty of other things. For instance, they want to know about any cargo insurance policies that you have as well as the efficiency of your billing department. Some of them are even more interested in the details of your business, such as the carriers and transporters that you use and your selection criteria. Even your communication skills need to be up to scratch. If you excel in all these departments, then your brand will be respected, and clients or shippers will prefer your services to others.

Business Development

Always remember to remain innovative. Try and find solutions that your clients need. Successful entrepreneurs are always seeking better solutions not just to beat the competition but also to improve service delivery. Your freight brokerage service could get to an entirely new level with more clients, increased cargo volumes and even high profitability. Remember, when you are proactive, you will grow and become more successful.

When you get started with your business, you will almost always feel like you never really managed to get everything done that you wished to. Fortunately, when it comes to a freight brokerage business, you will only need to focus on time allotment. Sometimes, your mind will be exploding with several bright ideas that you want to be implemented immediately, However, you may end up spreading yourself too thin which is never a good thing. There is a great approach that you can use which is known as the 80:20 rule.

Applying the 80:20 Rule to your Business

The 80:20 rule is also known as the Pareto principle. This principle simply states that 80% of outcomes will largely rely on only 20% of inputs. This means that about 80% of your income will most likely come from about 20% of your clients. This rule applies in numerous other situations in life. Simply put: 80% of what you can achieve will emanate from only 20% of what you focus your time, energy, and effort on.

To apply this rule to your business, you will need to figure out which aspects of your business can constitute the 20% of your precious time to produce the 80% of the results that you seek. This is something that you seriously need to consider because it will allow you to focus more on these activities so that you are more productive and can spend more time doing what matters. You will also ensure that you spend far less time on things that do not make you money.

Divide your Work into Categories

You need to divide tasks into several categories. This will make it easier for you to know where to focus more of your time, effort, resources, and energy. Some of the significant categories include:

- Operations
- Administration
- Sales and business development
- Marketing

Administrative functions: These functions are essential. They include processing paperwork, sending out emails, and handling human resources issues. If you have to go out and pay office bills or check mail, then you will be carrying out administrative functions of your business.

Operations: When you spend time managing your clients' needs, including cargo, making related phone calls and follow-ups, then you will be engaging in operations. For instance, getting loads from the system, contacting carriers, engaging with shippers, and even organizing to have cargo picked up are all considered part of company operations. Basically, when you engage in any activity that is directly related to accomplishing your clients' goals to deliver cargo, then you are engaging in operations.

Sales and Business Development: Sometimes you have to make calls, conduct some research and even visit a potential client. Other times you will be on the phone with your peers and other industry players hoping to acquire some long-term clients. All these activities can be considered as sales or business development.

Marketing: There are plenty of activities that we engage in that involve marketing. For instance, you probably reached out to shippers or clients to find new business. Maybe you put your business out there on different social media platforms to advertise your business. Perhaps you also sent out some Twitter messages or even prepared a marketing message on or e-mail campaigns. These are extremely important and most often than not, generate great awareness of your company's existence.

Using these measures puts you in a great position to make estimates about the amount of time you need to spend undertaking each activity. Try and note the amount of time spent on each activity. Now think about the impact of each activity on your bottom line. Is it possible to pinpoint the activities that have contributed to your revenues in a major way?

20% of Clients will Generate 80% of Revenue

If things follow the normal curve, then you can expect to generate 80% of your income from only 20% of your customers. This is a principle that has been observed and proven over hundreds of years, so it is better to align your plan with it than to oppose it.

To implement this rule effectively, you should consider applying the RMF rule. Using this rule, you will try and identify which clients have spent the most money on your services, which ones use your services most frequently, and which clients have most recently purchased your services.

Once you can identify these clients, zero in on them, and start focusing most of your time on them. If you prioritize these clients, then you will be building and reinforcing your revenue source. You should also spend some time identifying other customers who showcase similar traits.

Understand your Clients' Niches

Even after understanding which of your shippers have spent the most money or purchased services most frequently, you should invest your time into understanding other characteristics about your clients. For instance, try to learn more about the kind of industries they operate in, whether their businesses are seasonal or all-year-round and you will also want to understand where they are located within the country and if they require specialized equipment for their work. If you can figure out most of this information, then you will be able to understand your shippers better, and they will appreciate your efforts.

Access Department of Defense Loads

If you wish to access freight from the Department of Defense, then you should try and contact any carriers already in the system. However, your first step should be to register with FAK and with AA&E. AA&E stands for arms, ammunition, and explosives. Brokers can get onto the list of service providers by getting approval from the Military Surface Deployment and Distribution Command. Once you get approval, then you can easily apply for the numerous loads they have across most of the country.

Chapter 7: Marketing and Finding Clients

Now that your business is up and running, you need to begin marketing your firm and your services. There are various ways of marketing your firm. Some ways are better and more effective depending on factors, such as your location and so on. One of the best pathways to success is heading where others are not. This means delving into opportunities that others are not aware of and perhaps even avoiding where everyone else is headed.

Here are some of the things that you can do.

Create a Business Website

Clients always want to know whom they are dealing with. Since you are unlikely to get to meet shippers and transporters in person, the next best platform is a business website.

Therefore, take the time to create a professional website. This website should be informative, user-friendly, and presentable. It should have your official business name, a logo, and a clear indication that you are a freight brokerage firm. You need to let your potential clients know about your services, any specialization, experience, and even accreditations.

Crucial information that your website should display is contact information. Make sure that you include your address, official business name, and other contact information, such as an email address and phone number. If you have an official mailing address, include this as well.

Apart from these details, let potential associates, clients, and the public know about your exceptional services that can be tailored for different shippers. Talk about all the positive attributes, including affordable rates, reliability, efficiency, and so on. You want people to know just how professional and excellent your services are. As soon as your website is ready, let it go live, then start the optimization process.

Website Optimization

Now that your website is up and running, no one will know about it unless it is properly optimized. Optimization is the process of getting your website to rank high on search engines whenever anyone conducts a relevant search.

For instance, when shippers search for a reliable freight broker using a search engine, you want your website to appear on the first page of the results. This is only possible with SEO optimization. SEO stands for search engine optimization. You can learn simple SEO techniques or let someone else optimize your website for you.

Write a Blog

A blog is a personal website where you write whatever you want. Since you are in a niche industry, you can write about freight services and inform your readers all about your work. Within a short time, you will be identified as an industry expert. People will reach out to you for an opinion and advice. Shippers will want to be associated with you. A blog is, therefore, a great way to market your firm and let others know about your professional services.

Blogging is easy, especially when you are writing about something that you are passionate about. You can write about your experience in the industry and any challenges you may have encountered. However, your readers mostly appreciate informative articles that are full of advice and detailed in explaining aspects. Take time to write carefully and write in a manner that is easy to understand.

Make sure that you engage your readers. Provide them with an interactive platform where they can ask questions or post comments. A blog is an excellent marketing strategy that is easy to implement and effective over the long-term.

How to Get Clients for your Business

Your aim now is to get out there and identify paying clients for your business. However, it is easier said than done. You need to know where to go to find shippers. There are plenty of places you can try. For instance, you can consider the numerous shipper databases or directories.

These directories are filled with manufacturers' addresses. Many of them use brokers to move their products. The only challenge is that hundreds of freight brokers use these directories trying to reach shippers. This means it is pretty challenging to secure steady clients. Also, you will be required to pay about $1,000 to access the database. To be successful, you will need to venture where others don't and avoid places where everyone goes.

Initial Client Interactions

Ideally, the best way to make contact with clients is via the Internet. Once an online connection has been established, you can then move on to the phone. Therefore, your first interaction with your client will be via phone. The problem is that, on most occasions, you will be redirected to voicemail.

If you leave a message, then your recipient will most likely not return your call. If you are unable to get a callback after three or four calls, you may want to move on to your next client. Most shippers are very busy individuals with a lot of work to do. If you come across a potential client, simply inquire whether they use freight brokers or not. If they do, then this is your chance to pitch your services. Take the chance to show how different you are from others. Have some confidence and speak well without stuttering. If your potential client has questions, be patient and listen to them. Then proceed to answer the questions as clearly as possible. Remember that shippers have been in this business for a long time. They prefer talking to someone who knows what they are talking about. Therefore, do not beat about the bush; get straight to the point.

Diversification into Specialty Niches

The economy today is so immensely diversified that experts, such as freight brokers, can afford to specialize. When you start off, be open to engaging different shippers regardless of their loads. You do not want to lose out on any business.

Therefore, during the initial years, gain as many clients as you can and establish yourself. It is only much later that you will then decide to venture out into a specialty niche. Specialties can be very lucrative if you can be identified as an expert. This is because players in that niche will want to reach out to you, trusting that you will be able to deliver. Therefore, when the time comes, think about branching out into a specialty.

Although you will mostly be working from your home office, get some business cards. Business cards may sound outdated, but they come in handy when you are out and about. You will most likely bump into people who can help your business, so always carry some business cards. You may receive a call from a potential client when you least expect it. You can prepare some cards by yourself or pay a designer to do it for you.

How to Find Shippers

One of the biggest questions for new freight brokers is always where to find paying clients. This is an important question to ask, and the answer can determine the difference between a struggling brokerage and a successful one. The industry has developed immensely over the last decade or so. You can use freight broker software to carry out most tasks. However, the single most important aspect as a broker is finding clients for your firm.

As a freight broker and business owner, you want to find clients who will provide you with reliable, steady freight along lanes that you can cover. If you can find such clients and receive healthy margins, then you will be able to grow your business and live comfortably.

1. Consciously Observe the Brands around You

There are plenty of brands across the United States. They produce products that customers wish to purchase. Try and identify as many brands as you can in your neighborhood. If you wish to find shippers, then look at all the brands around you. Each brand is a potential client. The major brands produce products that are advertised and have to get to market.

2. Identify three new Business Contacts and Call them

Although it is never a good feeling, you should expect to lose a client occasionally. This is something that happens in every industry so do not be overly concerned. Due to this inevitable circumstance, it is smart to secure and call three different contacts daily. These contacts should be potential clients, so make sure that you contact them and see how it goes. Remember, if you only have one client, then your business will probably never get off the ground.

3. Do not Cold Call without Researching First

When you have a potential lead, don't call them before researching the company. If you call without any serious knowledge about a company, its operations or brands, then you could easily be dismissed, and they might not take your future calls. Research always impresses your caller.

4. Establish a Relationship

Once you make contact with a possible lead, try and establish a rapport. It is no secret that clients are more likely to buy from a friendly person than a total stranger. However, it's not easy to establish a rapport, especially when cold calling. The best way to do so is to talk about the client's lane or the volume they intend to move.

Other Ways of Finding Shippers

Observe other Companies in the Industry

If you have managed to get business with at least one company, then you should consider searching for their competitors. Find other companies in the same industry. You will probably come up with a number of companies. Research and find a way to contact them as they can be beneficial to you.

Observe A Company's other Branches

Suppose you already have a client in Fort Lauderdale, Florida. You will want to find out what other areas do the company operates in. If you notice areas where you have carrier relationships and the company has a presence, then this is a great place to source for additional business.

Check Out the Clients of your Client

You should also take a closer look at the clients of your client. Most major companies have many operations across different locations. If you deliver goods to one destination for further processing, then those goods will still have to get to another destination. Think about providing transport to that other destination. Since you are already a trusted partner, you could easily get additional business.

Co-Brokering and Double Brokering

For a long time, people have confused co-brokering with double brokering. However, there is a difference between the two. It is important to understand the difference because one is legal and one is risky:

Co-brokering: This is where you, the freight broker, accept a load from your client and then hand it to another broker to process and arrange transportation. It is legal and is acceptable.

Double brokering: This is the situation where a carrier accepts to transport goods on behalf of a client but then brokers a transportation deal with another company to transport the goods. In this case, the load has been double brokered.

Double brokering does not have any benefits; only downsides. It is also not allowed. On the other hand, co-brokering is acceptable and allowed. However, the original agreement between the parties sometimes specifies that either practice is not allowed.

Powerful Lead Generation Tips for Freight Brokers

1. Begin with people you know well or your current social circle.

2. I always advice new freight brokering professionals and companies to keep a notepad and paper handy in their vehicle for jotting down the names of companies they spot while travelling. Mention the name of the company, prominent landmarks, any contact information or anything else of special mention which can come handy in the rapport building process. You may note special information like they are the city's biggest paper manufacturers or a

fast food chain with the largest turnover in town. Get the idea? Anything notable and striking about the organization will do.

3. Grab plenty of leads on Thomasnet.com, Begin contact the customers on the Thomas.net database. There are literally thousands of prospects to target there. If you are uncomfortable with the prospect of picking from a random database, begin with an industry that you are familiar with. This will help you start and progress with greater confidence. You may have worked in a specific industry earlier, and may have a good working understanding of the sector. Start with it, and move on from there to cold calling other industries.

4. Research your drop off destination for consignments. Do a bit of research on the drop destination of your present load lot. Chances are there may be loads to be shipped from there. Plus, you'll probably be able to offer a more competitive price since you already have the transport logistics ready at the destination and don't have to organize any special transportation. To make the most of the trip to the destination, connect companies that may need moving consignment from there and offer them a reduced price. This way you'll optimize your resources.

Also, call the companies where your current load is being dropped off and ask beforehand if they have any loads that need to be picked up since you will anyway be having transportation ready after dropping off the consignment to them. You won't always hit jackpot using this method. However, at times, these companies may have their own load to drop off, where you can quickly seize the opportunity by offering them reduced shipping rates. Stay persistent when approaching these companies. They may not have anything for you at first. However, if you persist, they may just give you a one off order and then turn it into regular business if they are satisfied with your services.

5. Identify other shipping destinations within the same company. Say you've established a good working relationship with the shipping in charge of the shipping plant of the main company. However, the main company many have plenty of other locations across the country. These may also happen to areas where you've established carrier relationships. Use your networking and relationship building skills (hallmark of a good freight broker) to get your contacts to introduce you to shipping managers of different locations of the same firm. Get word of mouth referrals.

Ensure that you don't straight off ask your contacts for connections introductions. Be a little discreet and use your discretion. You'll need to do some fishing for on the phone and email to prequalify leads. Get a feel of your contact's rapport shipping managers of other locations.

You'll also want to feel out what your contact knows about the arrangements at the shipping location you would like to start getting business from. One of the best ways to establish connections is to pull out performance statistics from freight broker software, and paste them on a sheet out together by a professional. Find designers of Fiverr or Upwork at a reasonable price.

Chapter 8: Tips for Becoming a Successful Freight Broker

What are the things that distinguish an average freight broker who manages to break even from a successful freight broker? Here's all the actionable wisdom you need to know about being an ace freight broker.

1. Keep a varied and broad client base.

Keeping a diverse and broad client base is critical to being a successful freight broker. Losing out on one company or customer doesn't seem as heart-breaking if you have a ready database of several other clients to tap into. Top freight brokers understand the value of using a broader customer base so you don't depend on a single company for business. If one company who controls a huge chunk of your revenue moves their business somewhere else, you'll be in trouble. Therefore, even though you may have a few big customers bringing regular business, do not underestimate the power of building a broad client list.

2. Innovate

Another secret for acing the freight broker game is to be open to innovation and newer/more efficient ways of doing things. You can tap into other transportation related enterprises to avoid stagnation. I know freight brokers who have diversified into consulting other freight start-ups, purchasing trucks and becoming carriers. There's plenty of scope for diversification as a freight broker. You can be a one-stop shop for all logistics services. Many trucking company entrepreneurs start off as freight brokers. Keep innovating, adding new services to your business profile and expand your market to grow the business. Learn the ropes of the logistics and transportation business as a freight broker and then transition into building a transportation company.

3. Get rid of defunct carriers

Each trucking company has occasional service issues. However, if there are frequent lapses, you may have to take a call and drop the company from your database. If you are forever having issues with carriers, your clients will quickly move on to another freight broker or trucking company. Of course, initially you can't tell if a carrier is good or problematic. However, over a period of time you'll know the difference between trucks that offer good and snag-ridden service. While you can overlook a one-off case of transportation snag, set some boundaries before it starts affecting your business on a wider scale. Remember, it is not the trucking company but your reputation as a broker that is at stake here. If you enlist too many defunct and problematic companies in your database, it'll put your credibility as a freight broker at stake.

4. Preserve your reputation

The freight broker business is all about networking and building relationships/connections. Focus on building an enviable reputation within the industry if you want to go a long way. Don't take shortcuts or the easy way out if, it's even remotely shady. Have the integrity to pass it even if appears to be a huge opportunity. These things are noticed by people. Plenty of people need reputed, dependable and honest services. If you are able to offer it by keeping your vision firmly fixated on long-term goals, you'll increase your chances of acing the freight broker game.

Build your business on trust and integrity. Word can travel at the speed of a supersonic jet within the industry. Good or bad – companies will know what you are up to and make their business decisions based on your market reputation. One bad experience or one bad practice leading to court loss can damage your business. There will be tough times, and tough decisions to be made but if you want to sustain for long in the freight brokering industry, keep your integrity intact. Do it the right way. Avoid taking shortcuts or looking at quick gains and also focus on maintaining the highest service standards. This way you will increase your chances of having clients who are happy pay for good carrier services and want to associate with frequently.

5. Identify your niche

It is wonderful that you've started a freight broker enterprise. However, what niche are you going to specialize in? This is a good way to be a large fish in a small pond rather than a small fish in a large pond where there are several other fishes waiting for their share of profits. Find a clear niche such as dry van or frozen freight. Trucks and shippers operating in this niche will identify with your services, and you may end up getting a large chunk of profits in these niches. Specialized services will make your brand more sought after. If you are keeping your loads general, segment them effectively through various sections on your website or search function.

6. Join a professional association

Being an active part of any industry needs connections. Join the Transportation Intermediaries Association, which is a trade organization created for third-party logistics service providers.

You'll have plenty of professional contacts and networking opportunities. You'll also have access to education matter, top industry trends and codes on the best practices to be followed within the industry. Becoming a part of a professional association has multiple benefits. You'll get to know a lot of people from the industry and get business through referrals and word of mouth.

7. Never Stop Learning

Access to education is no longer a challenge, thanks to the internet. You can access online courses, free webinars, industry cases studies, podcasts, YouTube videos and virtually inexhaustible resources of information for upgrading your knowledge and skills within the freight brokering industry. These resources can help you stay within the industry loop at a marginal cost.

8. Keep in mind the 80-20 rule.

Keep in mind that there are plenty of administrative duties involved in the business of freight brokering. This can be everything from making invoices to maintain a company roster to drafting mails. However, as an agent, you'll need to stay focused only on income generating activities rather than spending a huge chunk of your time in administrative tasks.

Use the 80/20 Pareto Principle, which states that 80 percent of our results come from 20 percent of the input. This means only 20 percent of your activities are accounting for 80 percent of your total results. Use this principle to focus on those tasks that are producing those 80 percent results. Use this rule to also identify those 20% companies or clients that are contributing towards 80% of your output. It is common for 80% percent of a freight broker business' sales to originate from 20% of clients.

How can you use the 80-20 rule to maximize your profits?

First identify the activities that are leading to 80 percent of your sales and then invest more time in those activities. What are your main income producing activities? What are activities that boost your sales? In other words, you are identifying and channelizing those 80 percent activities that are driving more revenue to your enterprise. Maybe, seeking referrals, cold calling, attending networking events, visiting companies is what is doing the trick for you. Once you identify these 20 percent activities, spend more time doing them. This is one of the key secret approaches to growing your freight broker business.

Similarly, use this rule for customers. Identify your top 20 percent clients. These will generally account for about 80 percent of your company's sales. Direct a major share of your sales, promotional and marketing efforts on similar customers. Truth is, not all business activities and customers contribute equally towards the sales generated by your company. Some tasks are harder, others simpler. Some are more time consuming than others. Some have higher value than others. Learn to identify tasks that produce maximum value, and increase them. The idea should be to get good returns on your investment, including time and other resources.

9. Avoid rewriting the rules or reinventing the wheel

While it is good to innovate and diversify, if there's a system already in place don't reinvent the wheel. If you see a majority of successful freight brokers applying a using a specific strategy, service or marketing technique that seems to be working well, incorporate it into your business operations. You don't have to be unique and original all the time. Getting ideas that work from competitors, other freight brokers, logistics companies and truck carriers can lead your business in the right direction. Do what's working for others, and scaling it up with your own business sense.

At times, freight operators look to develop a brand new software system only to learn that there was already a system in place that catered to their needs. Don't waste time doing something different when people are getting results following an existing system.

10. Tone down the sales mode

I'll let you in on a little secret here that goes a long way in helping you gain a loyal customer base for your freight brokering business. Don't talk as if you are selling something. Tone down your sales pitch and speak in a more conversational manner, as if you are talking to family members and friends. Don't launch into sales mode as soon as you see your prospects.

Contrived/manipulated speech patterns, loud, exaggerated tones, slow and hypnotic sales inductions can get on the prospective client's nerves. Speak naturally and appropriately. Make it more conversational and relaxed so the prospect doesn't feel the pressure of doing business with you, which will end up making the prospect of associating with you less desirable. No one wants to talk to a robot who just wants to sell. People like a show of humanity and compassion.

Also, always stay in touch with your contacts. I can't emphasize on this point enough. Sometimes, freight brokers will simply stop communicating with companies or client's that refused their initial business proposal. Yes, they may have opted for another service over yours at the time. However, what's to say that they won't need your services in future. For all you know, they may be having problems with their current service provider or may need additional carriers. Staying in contact with potential customers ensures that yours is the first name that flashes in their mind when they need last minute or emergency bookings. As a freight broker, you'll get plenty of last minute businesses when shippers need carriers urgently. To bag these last minute deals, you have to make an effort to stay on top of the mind of your potential customers even if they have refused business deals in the past.

Send out festival greetings, keep checking periodically, send them messages about new services of features you've added to the business and offer a promo code or discount on the first shipment. Ensure you are the first name that comes to mind for last minute freight transportation deals.

11. Negotiations over the phone

Remember, as a freight broker, you'll have to negotiate plenty of last-minute deals over the phone, which is very different from face to face negotiations. Don't let a customer catch you off guard. Prepare well in advance for the negotiations by clearly knowing your terms. What are the typical statements you will sue to handle objections? What will you say to persuade your clients to agree to your terms? To what extent will you negotiate? Carriers may pose questions about the freight shippers or your customers are wish to move, for which you must have answers ready.

Keep your voice polite, professional and authoritative. Stammering or stumbling for words or appearing flummoxed at the client's questions doesn't help seal the negotiations in your favor.

Also, one of the most important things to keep in mind is while negotiating freight transportations deals over the phone is to stay alert. Do not try to multi task while you are speaking with a driver, shipper, traffic manager, dispatcher etc. Even something as simple as checking a mail can take your focus away from what the person is saying, which could result in a miscommunication, related to shipping terms that the other party may be requesting. Remove the risk of this pointless distraction and focus only on what the person is saying. Your calls and emails can wait until.

12. Take responsibility

Now, now yes you a freight middleman but that doesn't mean you go on telling customers that you are just posting their shipment, nothing else. Though it should be a given this unprofessional and unimpressive at so many levels, freight brokers still do it. What you are doing is telling the shipper that you don't have trucks for their consignment. You have to keep your posture like you are the trucking company that is responsible for transporting their shipment safely and promptly, and not just a middleman whose job ends after dumping the load in a truck. This approach won't help you get many repeat customers.

13. Be unfazed by the bigger firms

There are plenty of mergers, takeovers and acquisitions happening in the freight brokerage industry. This means small business and start-ups may start thinking about their chances among the big fish. How am I going to compete with these giants? Can my business survive after the latest acquisition that happened in town? You are a bee among the elephants. Moving, reacting and maneuvering become faster for you than large organizations with endless policies, codes and hierarchies. Make this work for you! You need a handful of good clients to do good business and spread a good work about your enterprise. The secret is to look at little known sources that the bigger companies won't change touch.

Bonus Chapter: Using Social Media to Grow Your Freight Broking Business

Like lots of other start-ups and enterprises freight brokers can also leverage the power of social media to grow their business. In today's age of smartphones, tablets and Wi-Fi, a huge chunk of your profit is left on the table if you aren't tapping in to the benefits of social media and doing business online. You build a steady community of loyal buyers who bring repeat business and more customers through word of mouth among their social contacts. Savvy businessmen are discovering the power of community in increasing their business and establishing greater communication with customers. Use slick digital marketing trends to draw more customers and reap rich profits in the freight brokering business.

The loads that are brokered to carriers may take several days on the road, however the impression you leave as a freight broken will be noticed immediately, which is why it is important to engage with potential and actual customers online. It helps you make a greater impact and stay on top of people's minds. Research has proven that brands that have a large social media presence have a higher recall value than brands that aren't active on social media. This is exactly why it is beneficial to have a strong social media presence online. Tap into channels such as mobile marketing, web-based applications and social media to further your business or have an edge over competitors.

I've often been asked how social media marketing can benefit the freight brokering industry, which is so un-sexy. It is only the interesting or sexy industries that can gather momentum from the social media (think food, fashion, lifestyle, travel). People couldn't be further from the truth. AA social media presence humanizes your brand. It helps any business (yes freight brokering included) establish connections with the audience and identify potential business opportunities. You can use the social media to engage your followers in a visual, casual and conversational manner. This leads to brand loyalty, and greater credibility for your business. You may miss out on a lot of business if you don't have a solid social media presence or network to connect with shippers and trucks/trucking companies.

These channels will not just facilitate the process of building your enterprise but also help you increase your brand recall value. A strong and easily accessible social media presence will also make it easier for your potential customers to research purchase decision, reduce the sales cycle duration and even prequalify potential buyers. There are plenty of digital marketing channels for streamlining customer acquisition and retention, in addition to upselling.

Having a strong digital media presence connects you to an increasing number of smartphone users. Currently, 91 percent of adults in the United States of American have access to mobile devices at any given time. This isn't just related to ecommerce or online shopping, but also actively seeking information and reviews about services. Have a clear, well-defined and unique value proposition that distinguish your services from those of other companies. Integrate your digital marketing to ensure that you have a powerful cross-channel marketing strategy that includes traditional media channels. Keep trying multiple approaches, while improving your efforts by reviewing social media marketing analytics or statistics periodically.

Here are some of the best social media marketing tips for freight brokers.

1. Use Facebook to Leverage Your Freight Business
If you don't already have a Facebook business page, here's why you should consider getting one pronto!
Over 467 million internet users are on LinkedIn. However, there are over 1.6 million daily Facebook users. Imagine the amount of opportunities and money you are leaving on the table for competitors if you don't have a strong presence of Facebook.
An average LinkedIn user spends around 17 minutes per month on the platform. However, an average Facebook user spends about 21 minutes on Facebook each day.
LinkedIn sees 3 new people registering on the channel each second, whereas there are more than 8 users signing up on Facebook each second.

2. Start by creating a professional looking business page for your freight broker business
Keep your personal and business page distinct by creating a detailed, visually aesthetic and professional Facebook business page. Click on the white down arrow to the upper right corner of your personal page to select the "Create Page" option.

3. Optimize your business page
Look at competitor's page or other freight broking firm business pages to understand how they've created their business pages. Review all the essential elements they've incorporated to optimize their pages for web and social media searches. Use elements such as banner images, a short yet compelling company bio, videos, images and whatever else you think will help customers like your business

and pick it over other freight broking firms when it comes to making purchase related decisions. Don't reinvent the wheel or start from scratch when you can easily emulate what other freight broking companies are doing. However, there's nothing that's stopping you from innovating and adding unique twists and interesting elements to your social media marketing campaigns.

Optimize the cover photo on your Facebook business page. It is the first thing people notice on your page and determines your digital media brand identify to a large extent. You can get a professional cover photo designed by freelancers on Fiverr. Keep your cover photo attention-grabbing but it should also be relevant, unique and interesting. Text can also be included in the cover photo. Write you company's tagline, slogan, mission statement, vision or ethics over the image if you are going to use the page more for branding. However, if selling online is your primary goal, a call to action can be more appropriate. Drive people to your website by including a call you action click through to the site.

Create an original, memorable and easily recognizable logo for the business, and use it across social media platforms to help customers easily recognize your business among several other freight brokering companies. Remember, your logo is your identity. Use it as the profile picture to help visitors recognize/identify your business quickly.

Keep your "About Us" section crisp, concise and on point. People in the virtual world have a short span of attention. They should be able to scan your "About Us" quickly to know more about the business. Use as many important, industry relevant keywords in the section as possible to optimize your page and make it more searchable when people are actively looking to connect with freight brokering companies on Facebook. Use words that resonate with your typical target audience rather than using industry heavy jargon. Highlight services offer by you along with details such as number of employees who work in the organization. Also, do not forget to include a contact number, physical address (will always lend more credibility to the business) and email.

4. Always link your personal account with your business page.

This is a wonderful way to alert contacts on your personal profile about your newly launched business, and get them to Like the business page for more exposure. These users will probably go on to share the content on your page, like your posts and engage on it to give your business greater traction. This could lead to multiple opportunities for potential business. More exposure translates into increased business opportunities.

To link your person and business page, begin from the personal page and click on the section the "Intro" option at the left corner. Then select "Edit" and add the name of your business. When it pops up, click on the button to add it. Once it becomes a link, people visiting your Facebook personal profile can visit your business page directly from your personal profile. This is a good way to get the word out there among your social contacts that you've launched a new business.

In addition, I've seen several savvy entrepreneurs post periodic updates about their business not just on their business page but also personal profile. This way you are targeting your personal contacts as well as people who've liked your business page.

5. Add the Facebook Fan box button on your business website or blog.

Okay, so now you've created a Facebook business page. However, don't you want visitors on your website or blog to know that you have a social media presence too? Wouldn't you want to stay connected to them and keep them updated about the latest offerings? One of the best places is promote your Facebook business page is your blog or website. You can also include in on your business card or brochure or email signature. Ensure optimum reach and exposure for your business by including information about your Facebook page. Place your social media buttons prominently on your web pages so users can easily like your content and pages by clicking on it.

6. Content is the absolute king

Engagement, interactions and connectivity is the most important element on social media. Power-packed content helps you accomplish these goals by increasing your credibility, authority and brand recall value. As a freight broker, you are acting as the middle man between trucking companies/trucks and shipping consignments, which means have a solid social media presence will help you stay connected to the parties involved for garnering greater business.

Keep in the mind the all-important "Rs" when you are drafting content for the social media. The first is – keep it relevant to your audience. Ask yourself if what you are posting is going to relevant or valuable to your target audience. Does it make sense to post healthy recipes on a page that is related to watches and other accessories? No, right?

Create content to position yourself as a social media influencer, authoritative figure, thought leader and expert in your domain. Speak in a lingo that is specific to your audience. Your fans should be able to relate to your posts, while also finding them interesting, informative and appealing. Remember, the golden rule of social media marketing, it is 80 percent making connections or building your brand and 20 percent selling. Avoid using your business page only to sell and promote offers. Instead, use it to make connections that will inspire loyalty and repeat purchases through continuous interaction.

People on social media will share anything that makes them come across as smart, intelligent and world-savvy among their contacts. They are simply looking to increase their social authority and impression. Give them something intelligent and share-worthy if you want your content to go viral.

Plenty of businesses make the mistake of limiting their social media content to promotional posts, thus missing the opportunity to build a brand and establish connections with customers to inspire loyalty. There are enough traditional marketing channels to push sales messages. The true purpose of social media is building trust, building a community around your business and engagement. Don't smother your fans with promotional content. As a thumb rule, follow this content ratio while drafting your social media content policy – 30 percent of the content on your social media page/account should be owned, while 50-60 percent should be curated. Only 10-20 percent should be devoted to promotional posts.

Keep updating content on your Facebook page regularly otherwise it runs the risk of becoming a ghost town. Content should be fresh and updated frequently. You can post anything from an industry specific article about the transport and logistics field or add your podcast or even a hilarious meme about the transportation industry.

One of the most important things to remember as part of the social media etiquette is to avoid posting anything negative or offensive about any religion, community, race, ethnicity or nationality. Stay away from offensive or questionable humor that can ruin your reputation as a business.

Remember, every post will go towards building your image as a freight brokering business. Before putting anything out there, ensure that it is accurate, well-researched and verifiable. You can also run contests or offer promo codes through your social media posts.

Engagement is the key to building a powerful social media presence. If you want more comments, posts and interactions from your fans, you must be responsive to them as well. It's a two way street! Make an effort to stay in touch with them and respond to their comments and queries promptly to make the interaction more personal and meaningful.

Give your audience something to discuss or chatter about in the comments section.

Streamline your content by using content scheduling and posting applications that will allow you to post a piece of content on multiple social media channels at the same time. You can create an editorial calendar and schedule your posts in advance to go on your business page/profile on a pre-specified date and time. You may not have the time to post on multiple platforms, in which case tools such as Hootsuite and Buffer come in handy.

Videos are huge today. Create an interesting, tightly scripted and compelling video about the shipping industry to wow your audience. Mention some facts, trivia or important information that they most likely don't know.

7. Post at the best time.

The best time to post on the social media depends on your industry and when your audience is most active. You can find out when there's more than usual activity on your business page by checking the insights tab on your page. This will give you all the information you need about when your posts are likely to be seen by your audience, what type of posts are gathering maximum response and more.

Sometimes posts where they have to select from one of the choices garner maximum response, while others times it can be an industry article or video. Use this valuable information for streamlining future social media marketing efforts to boost engagement and make your profile more appealing to fans.

8. Gather likes, fans, followers, and invites

You have a business page but it won't be impressive or credible until you have a decent following. There are several secrets for boosting your likes and fan numbers. Here are a few.

Start by inviting friends from your personal page using the "Invite Friends" option. This is quick and effortless. A lot of people on your personal profile already know you and will more than happy to like your page. Ensure that when people invite you to like their page, you return the favor so they stay loyal and connected.

Use your personal profile to join groups that are relevant to your business page. For example, as a freight broker, you can want to join groups related to trucking, freight, shipping and logistics, freight broker and other similar pages. Use these keywords in the search option and you'll get several groups related to your industry in the Facebook search result. Once you are a part of these groups, take time to go through their rules. Later, you can upload your content or share your posts on these groups or pages. Ensure you don't violate the group or page's rules or you'll get thrown out. Avoid posting if you aren't clear about the rules or check with the admin before posting.

9. Create Your Own Group
Smart entrepreneurs know the value of building and monetizing their own community. Build a community of loyal customers or potential customers by creating a group linked to your Facebook business page. You can promote the group on your personal and business page to attract more members. When people search for groups related to your industry, your group will pop in the search options. This way you are targeting people who are actively interested in being a part of groups that are relevant to your industry.

One of the biggest advantages of creating your own group is that you alone can set the tone and rhythm for the content that goes on the page. This is great when it comes to prequalifying potential buyers. You have a ready goldmine of interested and accessible buyers that can be used to build your brand (most important on social media), followed by promoting/selling your offers.

10. Build relationships

One of the biggest reasons why prospects convert into customers and existing customers convert into loyal customers is relationships. This isn't the same as a business or professional relationship, where prospects call you when the need for your product or service arises, and you fulfill the need. If all you are concerned about is doing business you'll keep targeting acquiring new customers all the time rather than retain existing ones. It takes much more time, money, and effort to acquire new customers than retain old ones; we all know this by now.

Thus connecting with your potential customers by establishing more personal and informal relationships in important. Get to know your prospective customers, relate to their issues and concerns, build trust and deepen your connection with them to the extent that they don't see you simply as a business. They see you as a humanized brand! When you engage your audience, they stop becoming a bunch of numbers of your prospect list. They become a loyal audience who trusts everything you say and depend on you to fulfill their freight service needs. You'll gain plenty of insights about your audience including their profession, relationship status, their hobbies and much more. Thus social media gives you the opportunity to connect with your audience on a personal level.

11. Handle negative reviews and comments like a boss

If you have a powerful presence on the social media and are also responding to customer queries and suggestions, chances are you will also attract your share of critics. Customers may leave a negative feedback, review or comment. How should you handle these comments as a freight start-up? Here are some tips.

Don't take negative comments or feedback personally. Yes, you may be the founder or owner of the start-up. However, that doesn't mean negative comments about your service are directed towards you. Avoid taking negative feedback personally and stay calm. Some customers will come up with genuine concerns and complaints, while others will simply pick fights for the sake of it. You have to stay logical, balanced and rational in all situations. Don't go guns and daggers on your customers at the slightest provocation.

Understand that people are simply reacting to their experience with your firm, not you. It is the business that is being reviewed, which isn't the same as commenting on you as a person.

Avoid getting into wrestling duels on social media even when you think a customer is being unfair or unreasonable. Your response should always be professional and polite. This stops the issue from escalating. You'll gain more respect from customer as a business if you keep it polite and professional.

Always acknowledge negative feedback and give your customers the assurance that they are being heard. The worst thing you can do for your social media reputation is to simply ignore negative comments and only choose to respond to the positive ones. If someone says the truck you tied up with didn't deliver the consignment on time, don't just move past the comment.

Instead, paraphrase the complaint to let your customer know you heard them out, and want to resolve this for them. Don't make excuses for shoddy service. Simply say, "I am sorry that it took the trucking company longer than expected to deliver your consignment." When you accept your mistake, the customer drops his guard down and you become instantly likeable to him. If you keep arguing and offering excuses, they get even more on the war path. Its human tendency! They'll probably have nothing more to say when you apologize and admit your mistake, and offer an assurance of better service in future. In fact, view negative feedback as an opportunity to convert the customer into a loyalist. If you handle it positively and professionally, you'll have a customer for life.

Don't create excuses such as oh! The trucking company was short-staffed or it was an exceptionally busy day delivering consignments. It makes customers even more annoyed. They've got nothing to do with the trucking company being short-staffed or busy. You only come across as someone who is shirking accountability and passing the blame to someone else. Just offer them a reasonable apology and assure them of better service next time. You can of course say something like, "this is uncharacteristic of us or this is an exception to the great service we always offer and we'd really like to make up for it". However, own your mistake by acknowledging it happened.

Add your strengths too while acknowledging the negative. Frame your response in a manner that addresses the customer's concern but also highlights your business' positives. "We apologize for the delaying caused in getting your consignment delivered. However, we've been successfully brokering consignments for several months/weeks now and serving happy customers across the city. However each customer is important. We would be happy to offer you [state reward or deal] to make up for the trouble" You aren't denying that the issue occurred or covering up for it. You are professionally acknowledging it, apologizing for it, yet highlighting the positives of your business and even offering to make up for it. This is the ideal way of handling customer complaints.

Conclusion

Thank you for making it to the end of this book. It should have been an informative guide that provided you with all of the tools needed to achieve your goals.

The next step is to implement the important lessons, tips, and advice you learned in this book. Remember that gaining knowledge is the most crucial step in setting up your freight broker business. However, it is how you implement what you have learned that will determine whether you will be a successful freight broker.

Therefore, keep on learning, consult with your peers in the industry, watch for new developments and always remain observant and positive. Remember to respect your clients once you get them, treating them professionally and with courtesy. If you follow the teachings contained in this book, you will soon be running a thriving brokerage.

If you found this book useful in any way, a review on Amazon is always appreciated!

Check out another book by Gus Bowen

www.ingramcontent.com/pod-product-compliance
Lightning Source LLC
Chambersburg PA
CBHW071417220526
45469CB00004B/1306